Dear Parent:
Your child's love of reading starts here!

Every child learns to read in a different way and at his or her own speed. Some go back and forth between reading levels and read favorite books again and again. Others read through each level in order. You can help your young reader improve and become more confident by encouraging his or her own interests and abilities. From books your child reads with you to the first books he or she reads alone, there are I Can Read Books for every stage of reading:

SHARED READING
Basic language, word repetition, and whimsical illustrations, ideal for sharing with your emergent reader

BEGINNING READING
Short sentences, familiar words, and simple concepts for children eager to read on their own

READING WITH HELP
Engaging stories, longer sentences, and language play for developing readers

READING ALONE
Complex plots, challenging vocabulary, and high-interest topics for the independent reader

ADVANCED READING
Short paragraphs, chapters, and exciting themes for the perfect bridge to chapter books

I Can Read Books have introduced children to the joy of reading since 1957. Featuring award-winning authors and illustrators and a fabulous cast of beloved characters, I Can Read Books set the standard for beginning readers.

A lifetime of discovery begins with the magical words "I Can Read!"

Visit www.icanread.com for information
on enriching your child's reading experience.

For Cara, the canine scholar in my life
—J.O'C.

For Rob—world's greatest vet and
best Pa of Ari and Oliver
—R.P.G.

To all the mutts and strays and pups
I'll never be able to adopt
—T.E.

I Can Read Book® is a trademark of HarperCollins Publishers.

Fancy Nancy: Time for Puppy School
Text copyright © 2017 by Jane O'Connor
Illustrations copyright © 2017 by Robin Preiss Glasser
All rights reserved. Printed in the United States of America.
No part of this book may be used or reproduced in any manner whatsoever without written permission except in the case of
brief quotations embodied in critical articles and reviews. For information address HarperCollins Children's Books, a division of
HarperCollins Publishers, 195 Broadway, New York, NY 10007.
www.icanread.com

Library of Congress Control Number: 2016949986
ISBN 978-0-06-237787-6 (trade bdg.) — ISBN 978-0-06-237786-9 (pbk.)

21 CWM 16   ❖   First Edition

Fancy NANCY

Time for Puppy School

by Jane O'Connor

cover illustration by Robin Preiss Glasser

interior illustrations by Ted Enik

HARPER

An Imprint of HarperCollinsPublishers

I am thrilled.

Thrilled means excited—only
fancier.

School starts soon.

I will miss Frenchy very much.

All summer

we played together.

I simply adore Frenchy.

Adore means love, love, love.

Frenchy is the best dog ever.

But sometimes she is naughty.

That means she gets into trouble.

Frenchy watches me

plan my ensemble for school.

Ensemble is fancy for outfit.

Frenchy wants to play

tug-of-war with my belt.

"No," I tell her.

"Belts are not toys."

9

Now I need to find my backpack.

Here it is!

It looks too small for me.

I grew a lot this summer.

11

I show my backpack to Mom.

Mom says, "We can buy a new one."

Then she runs into the kitchen.

"No," she tells Frenchy.

"You can't jump up on the table!"

The next day,

my mom and I go shopping.

I pick out a purple backpack.

At home

I tie ribbons around the straps

and make big bows.

I write out my name in jewel stickers.

Voilà!

In French that means "Look at that!"

Now my new backpack is perfect.

At dinner

I tell my parents,

"I am going to learn so much at school.

By the end of the year,

I may even be a genius."

(A genius is a super-smart person.)

I have to talk very loudly.

That's because Frenchy is barking.

She wants some of our dinner.

"No barking," my dad tells her.

"This is people food—not dog food."

After dinner I run upstairs
to get my new backpack.
I want to show my mom and dad
how fancy I made it.

Oh no!

Somebody pulled off the fancy stuff.

19

And I know who did it!

Frenchy!

"Frenchy, that was very naughty!"

I say.

Frenchy looks so sorry.

I give her a big kiss.

I really do adore her.

My mom hears me talking to Frenchy.

She sees what Frenchy did.

"You know what?

I think Frenchy needs to go

to puppy school!" she says.

Puppy school! Ooh la la!

Frenchy starts on Monday.

I let her wear my old backpack.

It is filled with puppy treats.

All the dogs are adorable.

That's fancy for cute.

We watch the teacher train the dogs.

Frenchy learns a lot.

By the end of the week,

Frenchy plays with only her toys.

She does not bark and beg for food.

Even at home

Frenchy leaves people stuff alone.

She really is the best puppy ever.

The night before school,

I get out my ensemble.

I put new ribbons

and stickers on my backpack.

Then I give Frenchy a kiss

and tickle her tummy.

"You were a very good student!

I am proud of you."

It's funny.

Frenchy is all done with school.

And I haven't even started yet!

Fancy Nancy's Fancy Words

These are the fancy words in this book:

Adorable—cute

Adore—love, love, love

Ensemble—outfit

Genius—super-smart person

Naughty—gets into trouble

Thrilled—excited

Voilà—look at that